The big yellow castle

Story by Annette Smith
Illustrations by Meredith Thomas

Katie and Joe
looked at the swings,
and the slide,
and the big yellow castle.

"Dad, can we go in the castle?"
said Katie.

"Away you go," said Dad.

"We can not play in the castle with the big boys and girls," said Katie.

"Come on, Katie," said Joe.
"We can play on the swings.
We will come back
to the castle."

Katie and Joe
played on the swings.

They looked at
the big boys and girls
in the castle.

Katie and Joe
played on the slide.

They looked at
the big boys and girls
in the castle.

"Look, Joe!" said Katie.
"The big boys and girls
are going away."

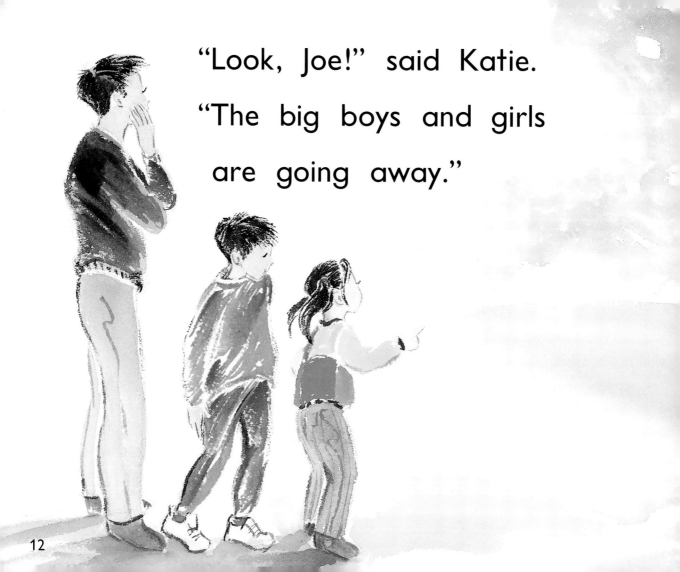

Katie and Joe ran
to the big yellow castle.

They went up and down,
up and down.

"Dad! Look at us!"

shouted Katie and Joe.